Differentiating
Instruction

Differentiating Instruction

A Practical Guide to Tiered Lessons in the Elementary Grades

**Cheryll M. Adams, Ph.D.
& Rebecca L. Pierce, Ph.D.**

Prufrock Press Inc.
Waco, Texas

Copyright © 2006 Prufrock Press Inc.

Edited by Lacy Elwood
Graphic Production by Kim Worley
Cover Design by Marjorie Parker

ISBN-13: 978-1-59363-197-0
ISBN-10: 1-59363-197-9

Library of Congress Cataloging-in-Publication Data

Adams, Cheryll, 1948–
  Differentiating instruction : a practical guide for tiering lessons for the elementary grades / Cheryll Adams &
Rebecca Pierce.—1th ed.
     p. cm.
  Includes bibliographical references.
  ISBN 1-59363-197-9 (pbk.)
  1. Individualized instruction. 2. Elementary school teaching. 3. Lesson planning. I. Pierce, Rebecca,
1950– II. Title.
  LB1031.A317 2006
  372.139′4—dc22
                            2005034749

At the time of this book's publication, all facts and figures cited are the most current available; all telephone
numbers, addresses, and Web site URLs are accurate and active; all publications, organizations, Web sites,
and other resources exist as described in this book; and all have been verified. The authors and Prufrock Press
make no warranty or guarantee concerning the information and materials given out by organizations or content found at Web sites, and we are not responsible for any changes that occur after this book's publication. If
you find an error or believe that a resource listed here is not as described, please contact Prufrock Press.

Prufrock Press Inc.
P.O. Box 8813
Waco, TX 76714-8813
Phone: (800) 998-2208
Fax: (800) 240-0333
http://www.prufrock.com

This book is dedicated to the many teachers and students with whom we have worked in appreciation for what we have learned from them. We also dedicate this book to our families and friends for their love and support.

Table of Contents

Introduction

At a time when many school systems around the world have embraced the inclusionary model to serve a diverse student body, it is vital that you, the teacher, have the necessary tools to teach in the inclusionary classroom. Little attention to diverse learners is given in content area courses or in-service workshops. This book will describe one model that provides you with the background and a template for designing lessons for diverse learners based on readiness, interest, or learning profile. These lessons address standards, key concepts, and embedded assessment.

Background

Research indicates that understanding individual differences among learners and knowing how to meet their needs is difficult for both preservice and in-service teachers. While teachers may want to do something to honor the diverse needs of their pupils, they may lack the skills and/or resources to do so.

Clearly, there is a need to provide teachers with tools that allow them to meet the needs of the academically diverse students in their classroom. Differentiated instruction is one such philosophy that allows teachers to respond to the needs of all learners. It is based on the idea that teachers need to adapt instruction to respond to student differences. Teachers may respond to differences in readiness, interest, and/or learning profile within the content (what students need to learn), the process (the way students make sense out of the content), or the product (the outcome at the end of a lesson). While there are a variety of strategies that are embraced by this philosophy, this book will present one strategy, tiered lessons, that, when combined with other essential elements, provides a model that allows teachers to implement differentiated lessons designed to meet an array of learner needs. In addition, the model addresses two themes often mentioned by teachers: the limited knowledge preservice and in-service teachers have concerning differentiation of instruction and differentiated strategies, and the perceived need to cover district curricula that prevents teachers from addressing students' differing needs.

What Is Differentiation?

Although differentiated instruction is not a new idea, the differentiation movement has taken center stage as a means of meeting the needs of all students in the classroom. Differentiation involves finding multiple ways to structure a lesson so that each student has an opportunity to work at a moderately challenging level. It is an organized, yet flexible way of proactively adjusting teaching and learning to meet students where they are, while helping all students achieve maximum growth as learners (Tomlinson, 1999). Instruction may be differentiated in content, process, or product according to the students' readiness, interest, or learning profile. For example, all of the students may be studying force and motion (content), but the laboratory experiments in which they participate may be at varying levels of complexity to accommodate their academic readiness for a particular task (process).

Successful differentiation will occur in the classroom when a number of essential elements are also addressed. These essential elements include specific classroom management techniques that address the special needs of a differentiated classroom, planned use of anchoring activities, a variety of differentiated instructional strategies, and differentiated assessment.

Chapter 1

The Model

Having worked with preservice and in-service teachers over the last decade on implementing differentiated instructional strategies in their classrooms, we have noticed several commonalities among teachers who are successful. As a result of this research, we have developed a model called Creating an Integrated Response for Challenging Learners Equitably: A Model by Adams and Pierce (CIRCLE MAP). The CIRCLE MAP, shown in Figure 1, is appropriate for any grade level and content area. It weaves together four elements—classroom management techniques, anchoring activities, differentiated instructional strategies, and differentiated assessment—that we found as the commonalities among teachers who differentiated successfully. Having observed teachers across the country and internationally, we consistently found these elements in classrooms that addressed the needs of all children. In our observations, good teachers try to incorporate higher level thinking skills, use structured alternative methods of assessment, and listen to students' opinions, but the same teachers often do not consistently use all four elements of the model. However, the classrooms in which we see exemplary differentiation occurring have teachers who use all four of the elements; spend much of their class time working in higher level thinking activities; deal with abstract concepts; use open-ended, student-directed forms of alternative assessment; and encourage students to question others' opinions and approaches appropriately. Next, we briefly discuss each of the elements of our model.

Managing time and space, flexible grouping, and individual work all require a clearly articulated classroom management plan. Students need to know and understand the rules for both individual and group activities. Anchoring activities provide meaningful practice, extension, or enrichment for students when they finish assignments and/or wait for teacher assistance.

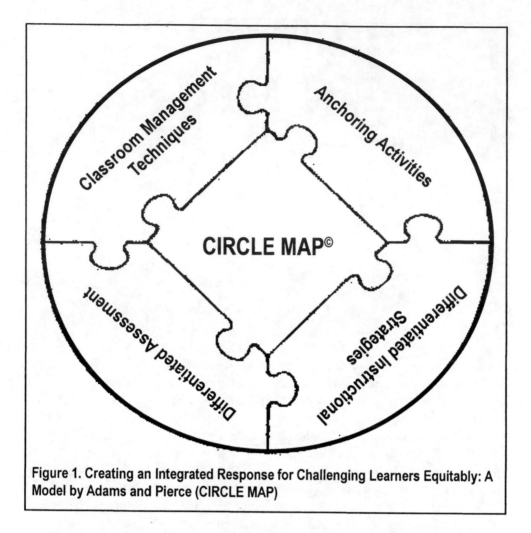

Figure 1. Creating an Integrated Response for Challenging Learners Equitably: A Model by Adams and Pierce (CIRCLE MAP)

A variety of instructional strategies such as compacting, contracts, cubing, and tiered lessons can be used to differentiate instruction. *Compacting* allows students to minimize repetition by proving their mastery of specific material. The student then has a block of time to work on self-selected or teacher-selected work while students who have not yet achieved mastery continue with the lesson. Often this "different" work is defined in a *learning contract* between the teacher and student. Both parties agree upon what is to be done, when it is due, and how it will be assessed. *Cubing* is a strategy that uses a cube as a means of presenting the learning tasks. On each face of the cube is a specific task that is introduced by a command word or phrase, such as "compare and contrast." For example, a cube that is used to provide review of the human body may direct students to "compare and contrast the nervous system with the circulatory system." Additional tasks would be printed on each of the other five faces.

Assessment should be formative, summative, or a combination of both. The teacher may observe the students as they share their ideas during a discussion and jot down notes for a formative assessment of each student. Summative assessments are given at the end of a unit or large block of study. The teacher could devise a rubric or may give a formal paper-and-pencil test. The form of assessment chosen should be based on the needs of the students and the lesson design.

This book focuses on tiered lessons, which provide different paths toward understanding a particular concept. No matter which path the student takes, understanding the concept and the essential understanding (the big ideas of a topic) should be the result. Because the lesson has been differentiated, the assessment may also be differentiated, such as using a rubric that has been adjusted to assess the product for each tier in the lesson.

Teachers often assume that differentiation of instruction means assigning students to heterogeneous cooperative groups in which the high-ability students become the "teachers," and the lower ability students become the "learners." When implementing the CIRCLE MAP, *all* students engage in meaningful work at a level that provides a moderate challenge for them. For differentiation of instruction to occur successfully, the teacher moves from being the dispenser of knowledge to a facilitator of knowledge, and the student moves from being the consumer of knowledge to the producer of knowledge. In the next few chapters, we will discuss each component of the model in detail.

Chapter 2

Classroom Management Component

The foundation of the model is the classroom management element. Anyone who has been in a poorly managed classroom for even a few moments understands that little or no effective teaching is taking place. Having no rules or procedures for classroom structure leads to a loss of instructional time, and student learning is compromised. According to Evertson, Emmer, and Worsham (2005), "Standards, rules, and procedures vary in different classrooms, but we don't find effectively managed classes operating without them" (p. 18).

Classroom Rules

Most teachers have rules for general classroom behavior, covering topics such as respecting others and their property, appropriate handling of materials, listening, and speaking (see Figure 2 for an example). It is important to phrase rules in a positive way. For example, use "Respect others' property" instead of "Keep your hands off other people's things!" In addition, students do better with a relatively short list of rules. As a rule of thumb, five to seven rules are appropriate for the elementary classroom. The classroom management component of the CIRCLE MAP must include rules for working in a variety of configurations. As the teacher, you can only work with one group or individual at a time. Therefore, we have found two critical rules that thwart chaos and preserve sanity. The first is, "Use 6-inch voices," meaning that students should modulate their speaking level so that their voices can only be heard 6 inches away. The second rule is, "Ask three before me." If students need assistance completing a task or come to a stumbling block in a lesson and you are not available, they should

---

Classroom Rules:

1. Listen carefully.
2. Follow directions.
3. Work quietly. Do not disturb others who are working.
4. Respect others. Be kind with your words and actions.
5. Respect school and personal property.
6. Work and play safely.

Figure 2. Sample classroom rules

---

find three other students to ask before they may interrupt you. If these students cannot answer the question, the student has permission to interrupt you. Adding the caveat that the student should also bring along the three students who were asked will nearly eliminate the chance that you will be interrupted except in extreme cases. It is a good idea to designate who the three "expert" students are for the day so students know exactly who to ask.

Flexible Grouping

Flexible grouping arrangements create opportunities to meet individual needs, which is the basis for differentiated instruction. *Flexible* is the key word. Students are rearranged for each lesson based on the lesson design and their individual needs. Groups can be formed in a variety of ways, including pairs, triads, or quads, as well as whole groups and small groups for instruction. Groups should be formed by both teachers and students, depending on the situation.

Teacher-Created Groups

Random assignments are easily achieved in a number of ways. A common way is to give each student a number and students with the same number will form a group. Another idea is to create a set of grouping cards using index cards that have stickers to identify each group (see Figure 3). Cards are shuffled and distributed to students, who then find other students with the same sticker and move to their preassigned area of the classroom.

How to Make Grouping Cards
- Decide on the number of groups you want (e.g., seven).
- Select appropriate stickers for your grade level with as many variations as the number of groups. For example, you could use smiley faces in seven colors or seven different kinds of animals.

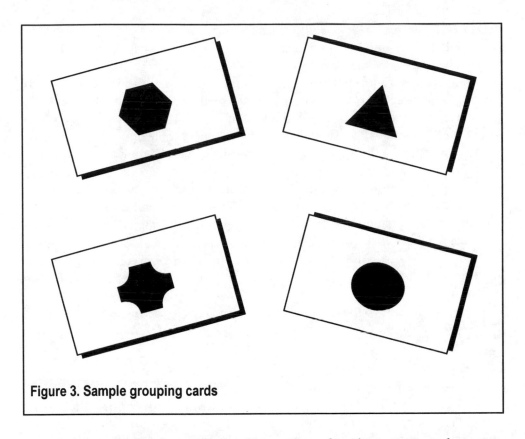

Figure 3. Sample grouping cards

- Obtain enough index cards for the number of students in your classroom (e.g., 28).
- Place one sticker on each index card and laminate, if desired.
- Decide where each group will work.
- Shuffle the cards and give one card to each student.
- Direct students to the appropriate area of the classroom for their group (e.g., you may have 7 groups with 4 students in each group scattered throughout the room).

To make the set more useful consider making enough cards to allow you to change group sizes as needed. At times you may want many small groups, while on other occasions you may prefer to have only a few large groups instead.

Sometimes teachers may choose to form nonrandom groups. Perhaps you want students grouped by ability, learning profile, or gender for a particular purpose inherent in the lesson. A convenient means of making groups based on ability is to circulate while students are working on the first part of a lesson and place a colored-ink stamp on the paper. Students then move to the appropriate groups for the rest of the lesson.

How to Use "Stampers" to Form Ability Groups

- Decide on the number of groups you want (e.g., you may want to have three groups: below average, average, and above average).
- Select appropriate "stampers" for your grade level with as many variations as the number of groups. Colored markers with the marker on one end and a design stamp on the other end work well.
- Provide all students with an activity to preassess their knowledge of a particular topic. For example, it may be a worksheet with a few problems about adding like fractions.
- Circulate as students complete the problems and stamp their worksheets based on the number of correct items. For example, students who do not seem to understand the concept might get a star stamped on their papers.
- Decide where each group will work.
- Direct students to the appropriate area of the classroom for their group.
- Provide reteaching, practice, enrichment, and/or extension activities for the groups.
- Work with one group while the other two groups work on anchoring activities (see Chapter 3).

Student-Created Groups

Occasionally allowing students the opportunity to choose their own groups is a good motivational strategy. These groups can be formed by free choice or by specific criteria set by the teacher. While free choice empowers students, it can also result in situations where some students may feel stigmatized. In other cases, excessive social interaction rather than task commitment may be the result. For these reasons be cautious in your use of this particular manner of creating groups. Using a specific criterion (e.g., groups of five or equal numbers of girls and boys in a group), while at the same time involving elements of free choice, sets parameters for forming groups. Because this method is not totally free choice, some of the issues may be lessened, but not eliminated.

As with any new skill, students may need to practice getting in groups in order to accomplish it effectively and efficiently. Students do not automatically know how to form or work in groups. It is important to provide opportunities to practice these skills before the students have to use them.

Keep in mind that when working in groups it is important for each student to have a specific task that is essential to completing the activity. One such system is BIGS: Boss, Investigator, Go-fer, and Scribe. The Boss is responsible for overseeing the activity. The Investigator manipulates any equipment or materials required to complete the activity. The Go-fer is responsible for obtaining and returning any supplies needed for the activity and is the only member who has permission to move around the classroom. Everyone else must stay seated or in the assigned area. The Scribe records any data and completes charts and other components of the activity. Keep groups intact until each member of the group has had the opportunity to perform each job.

Flexible Time and Space

A flexible use of time allows lessons to proceed to their natural conclusion rather than be carried out in set blocks of time. A lesson is not just something that is 30 minutes in duration; it may last for several days, where the richness of the activities dictates the amount of time spent on any individual day.

Arrange the desks or tables so that various configurations can be made to facilitate group work, as well as whole class groupings that encourage sharing of ideas. To maximize instructional time, some teachers have developed and posted various configurations for classroom furniture so students know exactly where to place their own desks (see Figure 4). For example, if your students are sitting in pairs and you want them to move to quads, the signal may be, "Move to Plan C." Plan C is posted on the wall and indicates the placement of each student's desk. However, for maximum efficiency, students have already practiced moving to Plan C in a minimal amount of time. John and Sasha know to move their desks to form a quad with Mary and Raul. At times this will form the group and these students will work together; at other times this procedure simply arranges the furniture and students are reassigned to quads as explained above.

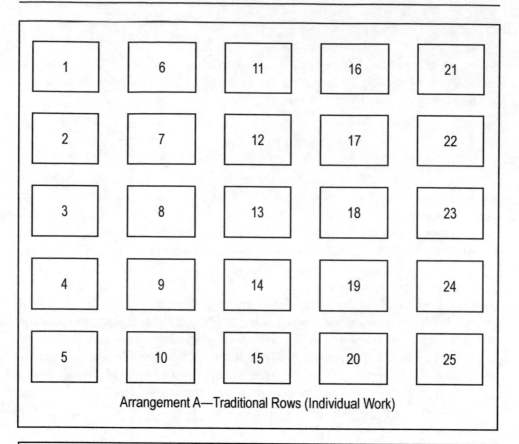

Arrangement A—Traditional Rows (Individual Work)

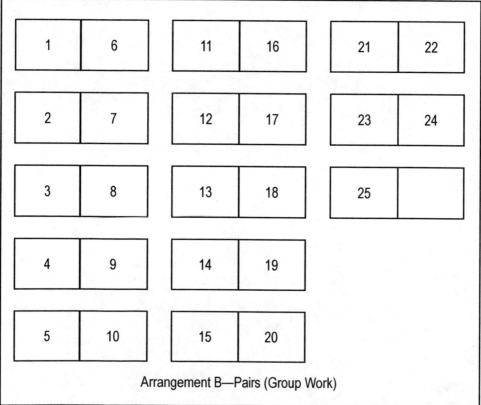

Arrangement B—Pairs (Group Work)

1	3	13	15	23	25
2	4	14	16	24	

5	7	17	19
6	8	18	

9	11	20	22
10	12	21	

Arrangement C—Quads & Triads (Group Work/Projects)

Figure 4. Sample classroom arrangements

Chapter 3

Anchoring Component

Anchoring activities, also called sponge activities, are provided for students to use when they are waiting for you to assist them before they can go any further, have completed their work and are waiting for you to begin the next lesson, or at the beginning of the class period to get them ready to work. Anchoring activities may be used before, during, and after instruction. These activities include relevant extension and enrichment work, individual assignments, skill practice, and teacher- and student-selected activities. Anchoring activities replace "I'm done" thinking with "What's next?" In classrooms where the CIRCLE MAP model is implemented, students know to move to their anchoring activities when waiting for the teacher's attention or when their current work is completed and the class is not yet ready to move as a whole to another lesson. Students know that it is always safe to work on an anchoring activity—they may be redirected later by the teacher, but they won't get in trouble when doing an anchoring activity. Anchoring activities foster autonomy.

Anchoring activities can extend the content by providing additional places to find the information. They can be used as skill builders. Sometimes students choose their own activities, while at other times the teacher chooses the activities. A wide variety of materials and resources can serve as anchoring activities (see Figure 5). A readily available source is a content-based textbook, which often has supplemental materials such as enrichment booklets, skill builders, and/or reteaching masters. Other examples of anchoring activities are brainteasers, crossword puzzles, 3-D puzzlers, listening stations, reading corners, activity folders, learning centers, differentiated worksheets, and pages from activity books dealing with the topic that is being covered. Because anchoring activities are not busy work but have specific purposes that tie into your lesson design and the needs of individual students, uni-

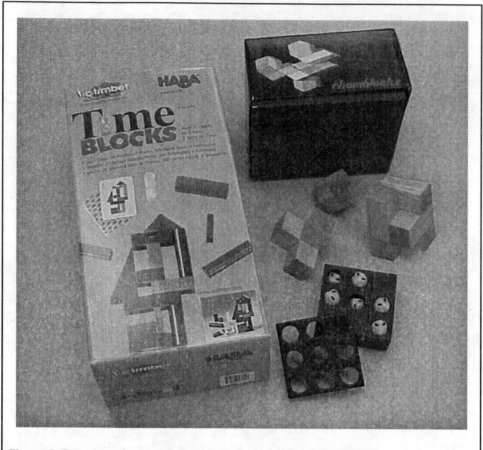

Figure 5. Samples of commercially produced anchoring activities

versal examples are not appropriate. However, Chapter 8 contains further information about sources for anchoring activities for a variety of subjects.

There are a number of ways to organize anchoring activities. Some teachers provide individual file folders for each student and periodically place appropriate activities in the folder. Others have a specific area of the classroom designated for the storage and use of the anchoring activities. One of the most creative ideas we have seen uses an over-the-door shoe bag that hangs on a closet door (see Figure 6). In each shoe pocket is an anchoring activity. Students select an activity from a pocket and replace it when they are finished. Several teachers we know have created eye-catching bulletin boards using anchoring activities and have placed necessary materials to complete the activities in boxes on shelves under the bulletin board.

Although you may choose to grade some or all of the anchoring activities, their primary purposes are to extend the curriculum, encourage skill building, provide choice and challenge, and foster autonomy. In addition, while you are working with

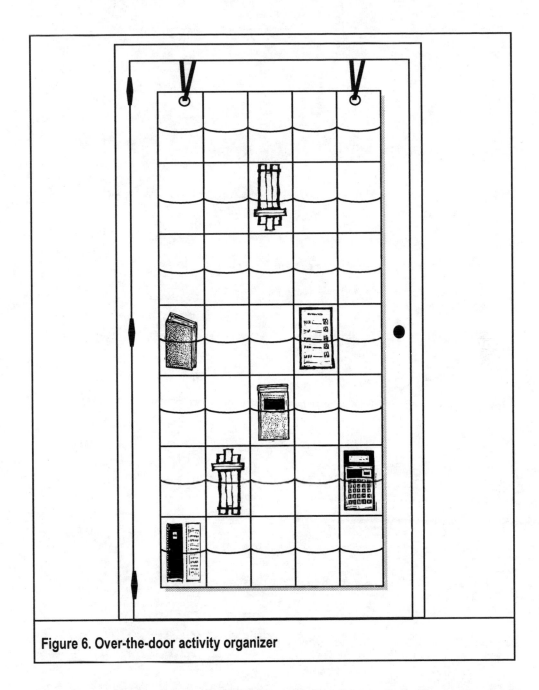

Figure 6. Over-the-door activity organizer

one group, the other students need to have activities that will challenge them and allow them to work independently until it is their turn for your attention. Anchoring activities help keep the differentiated classroom from becoming chaotic.

Chapter 4

Differentiated Instructional Strategies Component

There are a wide variety of instructional strategies that can be used to differentiate instruction, but the focus of this book is on a specific strategy—tiered lessons. Tomlinson (1999) describes tiered lessons as "the meat and potatoes" of differentiated instruction. A tiered lesson is a differentiation strategy that addresses a particular standard, key concept, and essential understanding, but allows several pathways for students to arrive at an understanding of these components, based on the students' readiness, interests, or learning profiles. Lynn Erickson (2000) describes essential understanding as "the key principles and generalizations that develop from the fact base . . . They are the 'big ideas' that transfer through time and across cultures" (p. 47).

Tiering by Readiness

A lesson tiered by readiness level implies that the teacher has a good understanding of the students' ability levels with respect to the lesson and has designed the tiers to meet those needs. Think of a wedding cake with tiers of varying sizes (see Figure 7). Many examples of lessons tiered in readiness have three tiers: below grade level, at grade level, and above grade level. There is no rule that states there may only be three tiers, however. The number of tiers depends on the range of ability levels in the classroom. Remember: You will be forming tiers based on your assessment of your students' abilities to handle the material particular to the lesson. Students are regrouped when you move to a different lesson.

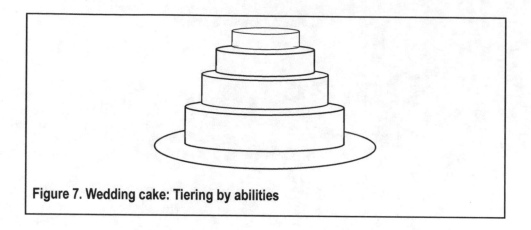

Figure 7. Wedding cake: Tiering by abilities

Tiering by Interest or Learning Profile

When the lesson is tiered by interest or learning profile, the teacher is look-ing at student characteristics other than ability level. For example, the lesson might be tiered to focus on three learning styles: auditory, visual, and kines-thetic. Students would then be placed in the tier that best matches their learn-ing style and their ability levels will be varied. In these instances, all students are given choices of content, process, or product that are at about the same level. These tiers are similar to those in a layer cake—all the same size (see Figure 8).

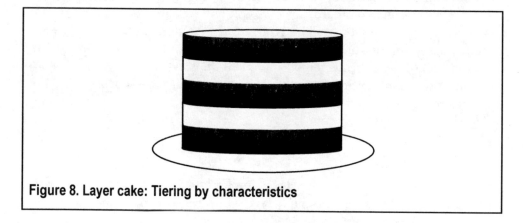

Figure 8. Layer cake: Tiering by characteristics

Forming Tiers

The number of groups per tier will vary, as will the number of students per tier. Do not try to form groups of equal size; instead, groups should be formed based on the readiness needs of individual students. For example, Tier One may have two groups of three students; Tier Two, five groups of four students; and Tier Three may have one group of two students. When the lesson is tiered by interest or learning profile, the same guidelines apply for forming groups—different tiers may have varying numbers of students. Even if students are already grouped into classes by ability, there is still variability at each ability level, and teachers still need to address the varied ability levels in each population.

Creating a Tiered Lesson: Step-by-Step

When developing a tiered lesson, we have found the nine steps described below useful.

1. Identify the grade level and subject for which you will write the lesson.
2. Identify the standard (e.g., national, state, and/or local) that you are targeting. A common mistake for those just beginning to tier is to develop three great activities and then try to force them into a tiered lesson. Start with the standard first. If you don't know where you are going, how will you know if you get there?
3. Identify the key concept and essential understanding. The key concept follows from the standard. Ask yourself, "What 'Big Idea' am I targeting?" The essential understanding follows from the concept. Ask yourself, "What do I want the students to know at the end of the lesson, regardless of their placement in the tiers?"
4. Develop a powerful lesson that addresses the essential understanding. This will be the base from which you develop your tiers.
5. Identify the background necessary to complete the lesson and be sure students have this necessary information to be successful in the lesson. What scaffolding is necessary? What must you have already covered or what must the student have already learned? Are there other skills that must be taught first?
6. Determine which element of the lesson you will tier. You may choose to tier the content (what you want the students to learn), the process (the way students make sense out of the content), or the product (the outcome at the end of a lesson, lesson set, or unit—often a project). When beginning to tier, we would suggest that you only tier one of these three. Once you are comfortable with tiering, you might try to tier more than one part of the same lesson.
7. Determine the type of tiering you will do: readiness, interest, or learning profile. Readiness is based on the ability levels of the students. Preassessing is a good way to determine readiness. Interest is based on their attraction to a topic, generally gauged through an interest survey. To preassess students' interests, a teacher might design an interest inventory listing several topics that students will be studying or several activities that the teacher is considering using. Students can rank-order their choices and the teacher can use the rankings to assign students

to groups based on their choices. Learning profile may be determined through various learning style inventories. There are a variety of instruments to determine a student's learning profile. Two good interactive instruments may be found on the Internet at http://www.ldpride.net.

8. Determine how many tiers you will need based on the choices above and develop the lesson. If you choose to tier based on interest or learning profile, you may control the number of tiers by limiting choices (using only a few different learning styles). Tiering on all eight of Gardner's multiple intelligences (Campbell, Campbell & Dickinson, 2003) in one lesson may not be a good place to start! For example, choose logical-mathematical intelligence, spatial intelligence, and verbal-linguistic intelligence.

   Tiering can apply to nearly every facet of a lesson. For example, in a science laboratory lesson, students may have done some very simple investigations using observation and inference and formed conclusions based on data. Most activities were probably teacher-led with fairly predictable results. Now the teacher is ready to have different groups do different experiments that are more open-ended. Students are given a pretest to determine their placement. Students who have a good understanding of observation and inference, but need help with other science process skills should be placed in the basic, or first, tier. Students who understand observation, inference, and prediction and have some concept of controlling variables should be placed in the grade level, or second, tier. Those who show mastery of the basic science process skills should be placed in the advanced, or third, tier. At each tier, the teacher may choose to leave the activity open or provide more structure by adding specific directions. Students in the first tier will need the most assistance with experimental design and the actual carrying out of the investigation. The third (advanced) tier should be able to figure out what they need with few additional directions, and the second (grade level) tier will be somewhere in between, depending on the students in that tier.

9. Determine the appropriate assessment(s) you will use based on your activities. Both formative and summative assessments may be included in the lesson. See Chapter 5 for more detail about assessment.

Differentiation means doing something different—qualitatively different. Make sure you keep this in mind when tiering the lessons. The key word here is *qualitatively* as opposed to quantitatively different. What you don't want to have happen is that students' tiers differ in the *amount* of work they have to do rather than the *kind* of work they do. Secondly, be sure each tier is doing moderately challenging and developmentally appropriate work. In other words, no group should be given "busy work." One group should not be doing blackline practice sheets, while another does a fabulous experiment.

Chapter 5

Differentiated Assessment Component

Don't confuse the terms *assessment, evaluation,* and *grading.* Assessment is the gathering of data, evaluation refers to the judging of merits, and grading is assigning values to letters or numbers for reporting purposes (Rolheiser, Bower, & Stevahn, 2000). We will discuss issues related to assessment because schools usually have their own policies concerning evaluation and grading that are not at each teacher's discretion to arbitrarily change or modify.

Assessment should be formative, summative, or a combination of both. In a differentiated classroom, teachers are constantly studying their students. They gather data in every lesson through a variety of means, both formal and informal. Therefore, assessment is an integral part of every lesson and informs the learning process.

Formative Assessment

Teachers in a differentiated classroom don't wait until the end of a unit or chapter to determine what students do or don't know. Student-teacher conferences, exit cards, journaling, small group interviews, graphic organizers, and surveys are all informal means of assessment that allow the teacher to get a picture of where the students are in their learning. This information is then used to adjust or design further learning experiences. Because you are already familiar with student-teacher conferences, small group interviews, and surveys, we briefly describe other examples of formative assessment next.

Exit cards or tickets to leave are used to gather information about the day's lesson. Teachers may use index cards or slips of paper with predetermined prompts. Students respond to the prompts and turn in their answers as they leave the classroom before lunch or recess or at the end of the day. You should review the cards to determine how to adjust the lesson. The cards allow you to readily see who is still struggling with the topic and who has grasped the material. A teacher may distribute pieces of paper similar to the following example:

EXIT CARD

Today you began to learn about improper fractions.

- List three things you learned.
- Write at least one question you have about improper fractions.

Journaling is another way to capture students' understanding in a written or graphic form. Students may have a specific journal for each subject or a single journal in which they keep all of their ideas. Students respond to a predetermined prompt that the teacher provides verbally or by writing on the blackboard. For example, if the class has been studying the life and work of Dr. Martin Luther King, Jr., the teacher could instruct the students to open their journals and respond to the following prompts:

- List three important events in Dr. King's life.
- Write two questions you would ask Dr. King if you could talk to him.
- Name one way you are similar to Dr. King.

Graphic organizers provide a visual means of representing concepts, facts, and principles to convey students' conceptual understanding of a topic. They come in a wide variety of forms and can be used for any subject. Through these effective, content-oriented visual tools, teachers can reinforce key concepts and develop critical-thinking, organizational, and writing skills in their students, as well as inform their instruction.

For example, a simple graphic organizer that may be used in any subject is the Venn diagram, which is illustrated using plant and animal cells (see Figure 9). Some teachers use flip cards, and others use sticky notes or printed labels attached to a clipboard. For a formative assessment, the teacher may observe the students as they share their answers during a discussion and jot down notes for a formative assessment of each student. The teacher may ask him- or her-

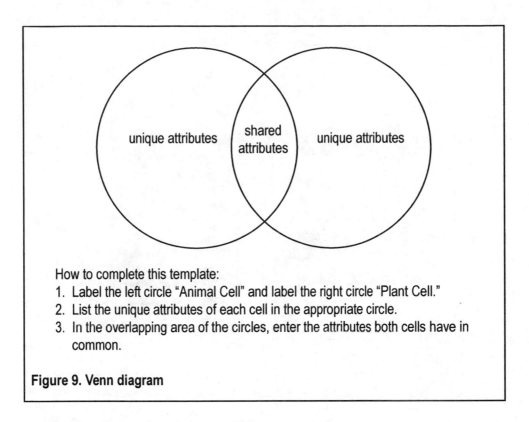

How to complete this template:
1. Label the left circle "Animal Cell" and label the right circle "Plant Cell."
2. List the unique attributes of each cell in the appropriate circle.
3. In the overlapping area of the circles, enter the attributes both cells have in common.

Figure 9. Venn diagram

self, which child is struggling with the concept? Which child is moving rapidly and accurately through the material? Whose answers show more thought and insight? The teacher may use some means of recording these observations of the various groups. Our favorite method is the flip card chart, which can be created economically using a file folder, index cards, and clear tape.

Here are the instructions for creating a flip card chart for formative assessment (see Figure 10):

- Select a file folder.
- Select two colors of 3" x 5" or 4" x 6" index cards. For example, with 24 students, you could select 12 white cards and 12 blue cards.
- Determine how you will alphabetize the cards in the file folder (i.e., top down, bottom up, first name or last name, separated by gender, or another method).
- Write the name of each student on an index card by holding the index card so that the top margin is toward you. Lined index cards provide ease of writing names, as well as placement in the file folder. Keep in mind that you will want the names to be on alternating card colors.
- Determine how many cards will be taped to each side of the file folder. Using 3" x 5" cards will allow a maximum of 17 cards per side of a standard file folder.

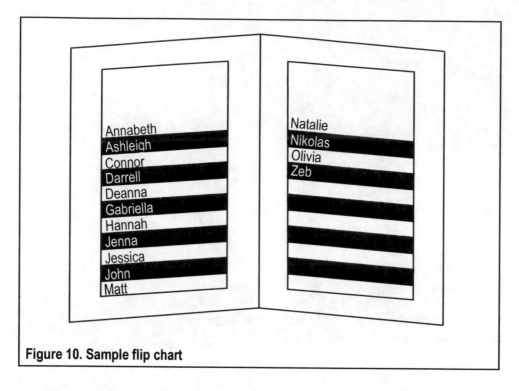

Figure 10. Sample flip chart

- Take one index card and tape it onto the inside of the file folder so that the name is facing outward at the bottom of the folder.
- Place the next index card in the alternate color with its edge overlapping with the first card so that only the name is showing on the first card.
- Continue to place and tape alternating colors of index cards in the same way until one side is full.
- Repeat the process of placing and taping cards for the other side of the file folder.

This device can be used effectively when students are working in groups, during whole group discussions, and completing individual seatwork. As students work in groups, you, holding the folder in one hand and a pen in the other, should circulate among the students and record observations and/or anecdotes on each student's card to assess student progress. Similarly, as you facilitate a whole group discussion, the flip chart can be placed on a podium or your lap for making note of particularly thoughtful answers, creative insights, and/or misconceptions. Likewise, during individual seatwork, notes can be made as you circulate among the students.

Summative Assessment

Culminating or summative assessments are given at the end of a unit or large block of study. These are typically used for evaluation and grading, as well as to inform the learning process. What will be assessed determines the method of assessment.

If students are creating a product, the teacher can develop a rubric for that particular product. Rubrics should be shared with the students when the product is assigned. Rubrics should go beyond a checklist and designate at least three levels of performance (e.g., novice, distinguished, and expert). See the resource list for information about software and texts for creating rubrics for a wide variety of products.

To create your own analytic rubric from scratch for a particular product, follow these steps:

1. In a chart, list along the left hand side the essential criteria (i.e., facts, skills, and/or concepts) you will assess; a manageable number is six or fewer.
2. Across the top of the chart, list the number of levels to be used for the rubric (e.g., novice, distinguished, expert; remedial, average, advanced; or 1, 2, 3, 4).
3. Write descriptions for each square of the chart; begin by describing the desired result and adjust the description for each of the other levels.
4. Assign points to each level that will allow you to distinguish between types of student work.

As you use the rubric and reflect on your students, you may wish to revise and fine tune the details.

Illustrated on the following page is a rubric used to assess students' cell models that were created for their science class (see Figure 11). Note that there are 3 criteria and 6 levels, with 2 points assigned to each level for a maximum total of 30 points.

The teacher may give a formal paper-and-pencil test that has a core block of questions that all students must attempt and a block of questions from which students can select the specific ones they will answer to accumulate the necessary points. For example, on a test with 100 points, all students have to answer the core portion that equals 75 points and then select the remaining 25 points from a bank of questions of varying point value and difficulty level.

Alternative assessments, such as portfolios, projects, and other more authentic tasks can also be used for formative or summative assessment. Portfolios take many different forms but usually consist of a compilation of student work under specific guidelines. What is important, however, is the purpose of the portfolio—who is the audience, how will the portfolio be used by teachers and students, and what are the benefits to the student? One of the main advantages of using portfolio assessment is that students learn to judge their own work and the progress they are making. See the resource list in Chapter 8 for an extensive list of materials to use in learning about or constructing your own authentic tasks and projects. The form of assessment you choose should be based on your needs and lesson design.

Criteria	0 Points	2 Points	4 Points	6 Points	8 Points	10 Points
Animal or plant cell created with nine organelles included in the model with correct function and structure	No Product	2–5 organelles represented realistically in cell	6–7 organelles represented realistically in cell, or 1–2 organelles appear unrealistic	8–9 organelles represented realistically in cell, or 1 organelle appears unrealistic	9 organelles represented realistically in cell in structure and function	Wow! Exceptional detail present, making cell look very realistic
Product shows knowledge and understanding of cell organelles' function and structure	No Product	Correct structure only—no function	Correct structure and some functions correct	Understanding apparent for the most part, function and structure correct	Good understanding of both function and structure	Wow! Very evident understanding of both function and structure
Creativity/Originality	No Product	Shows little creativity and originality	Shows some creativity and originality	Shows many creative and original ideas, some extra details added	Elaborate and original, many extra details or props present	Wow! Exceptional creativity and originality

Figure 11. Rubric for cell model

Chapter 6

Tiered Lesson Example

Tiered lessons may be described briefly as a way to have students address the same academic standard or concept, but at varying levels of complexity or structure. In our tiered lesson template, the teacher always begins with the subject, grade, and standard (national, state, and/or local). Secondly, the teacher indicates the key concept and the essential understanding. Teachers choose to modify the content, process, and/or product in the lesson, according to students' readiness, interests, and/or learning profiles. The lesson is then differentiated to provide various tiers, or paths, that lead students toward an understanding of the concept and essential understanding.

Tiered Lesson Basics

To take a closer look at the anatomy of a tiered lesson, we have included a science lesson (see Figure 12) and detailed how the nine steps discussed in Chapter 4 were used to develop the lesson we've included. Notice that all three tiers are working on the same standard, concept, and essential understanding. Students in each tier have a different book to read from the other tiers, each tier works with the content in the same manner, and all students produce the same product. Tier I is the lowest level; Tier III is the highest level.

The following steps show how we applied the nine steps for creating tiered lessons to a science lesson.

1. Identify the grade level and subject for which you will write the lesson. In our example, the grade level is third and the subject is science.

Subject: Science

Grade: Third

Standard: Content Standard C: Students will develop an understanding of organisms and environments.

Key Concept: Organisms react to environmental change.

Essential Understanding: Organisms depend on their environment, where changes occur; some of these changes are caused by the organisms themselves.

Background: This is one piece in a unit on environments and will introduce the concept of reactions to environmental change. In each story there is a focus on a particular environment or series of environments. For each tier, the students will read the assigned book (or listen if the story is taped for struggling readers who comprehend at a level higher than they can read).

Tier I: These students will read *Bringing the Rain to Kapiti Plain* (Aardema, 1981).
Tier II: These students will read *The Desert Is Theirs* (Baylor, 1975).
Tier III: These students will read *The Story of the Jumping Mouse* (Steptoe, 1972).

Whole Group Process: Students will choose three characters in the story and describe in pictures or writing how the changes in the environment(s) affected each character with respect to their basic needs. The teacher will then initiate a discussion using shared inquiry where the students sit in a circle so that they can make eye contact with each other and the teacher. The teacher has prepared a seating chart for the circle so that she can keep track of student responses and interactions. The teacher begins by asking an interpretive question such as, "Why do you think some animals migrate and some animals don't?" Students will have an opportunity to share what they learned and substantiate their point of view from their individual readings. In addition, they will look for similarities and differences across the different environments, paying particular attention to how the organisms changed their environments and how the environment changed the organisms. The question is resolved when all possible interpretations are before the group.

Whole Group Long-Term Product: Students may choose to design and paint a mural to hang on one wall in the classroom to depict the various environments they studied.

Assessment: The teacher will note the students' responses during sharing and check their drawings/writings for accuracy.

Figure 12. Science lesson tiered in content according to readiness

2. Identify the standard (national, state, and/or local) that you are targeting. The author of this lesson has selected Content Standard C: Life Science of the National Science Education Standards (NRC, 1996).

3. Identify the key concept and essential understanding. In this example, it is an understanding of reaction to change. The essential understanding follows from the concept. In this lesson, all students will come away knowing organisms depend on their environment, where changes occur, and that some of these changes are caused by the organisms themselves.

4. Develop one lesson. This lesson was developed using the book *The Story of Jumping Mouse.*

5. Be sure students have the background necessary to be successful in the lesson. Before engaging in this lesson, students have studied some basic vocabulary and an introductory chapter on basic needs of living things as part of an environmental unit.

6. Determine the area in which you will tier the lesson. This lesson is tiered in content. For this lesson, students are placed in one of three tiers based on their ability to comprehend what they have read or what has been read to them. We are making a distinction here between reading level and comprehension level. We have found that many students who have learning disabilities in the area of reading can comprehend at a much higher level when the material is read to them or they listen to it on tape. *Bringing the Rain to Kapiti Plain* (Aardema, 1981) is an engaging book with beautiful illustrations. It is an African folktale and is retold in the same meter as "This Is the House That Jack Built." The repetition and illustrations are helpful for those students who have difficulty comprehending grade level material. *The Desert Is Theirs* (Baylor, 1975) is more abstract than *Bringing the Rain to Kapiti Plain*. Students must make more inferences in their comprehension of the material. The third book, *The Story of Jumping Mouse* (Steptoe, 1972), involves more than one biome, while each of the other two books only deals with one biome.

7. Determine the type of tiering you will do: readiness, interest, or learning profile. In this lesson, the author chose readiness. The content in the book for each tier beginning in Tier I and moving through Tier III differs from simple to complex and from single facet to multifaceted, to use Carol Tomlinson's Equalizer word pairs (see Figures 13 and 14 on pages 33 and 34). The Equalizer is a chart with nine pairs of words or phrases, such as *more structured-more open* and *concrete-abstract*. The word in each pair that describes the least complex idea is listed on the left hand side and the other word is listed on the right. The idea is to slide a "lever," similar to the equalizer on a stereo, to assist the teacher in finding the point of "best fit" between a task and a particular student (Tomlinson, 1999). Tier I is the lowest level; Tier III is the highest level.

8. Based on your choices above, determine how many tiers you will need and develop the lesson. Make sure that all the tiers have challenging, meaningful, and engaging activities and the activities in one tier do not look more appealing than another.

9. Based on your activities, determine the appropriate assessment(s) you will use. In this lesson, the teacher notes the students' responses during sharing with her flip card chart and checks their drawings/writings for accuracy.

One Final Note

Time, energy, and patience are required to learn to effectively differentiate instruction in an academically diverse classroom. In addition, teachers need administrative and peer support, as well as professional development over extended periods of time—you won't have a differentiated classroom the day after reading this book. Start small; choose a favorite lesson in your next unit and tier it according to the needs of your students. Seek the expertise of specialists, such as special and gifted education coordinators, media specialists, and others to collaborate to improve instruction in the academically diverse classroom.

Remember all the components of the CIRCLE MAP are essential. To be successful you will need to integrate and implement all four components—the classroom management techniques, the anchoring activities, differentiated instructional strategies, and differentiated assessment. This is especially true when using tiered lessons. We can guarantee success only if you implement all four components. Having a classroom with all the components in place will empower you and your students to maximize teaching and learning for all.

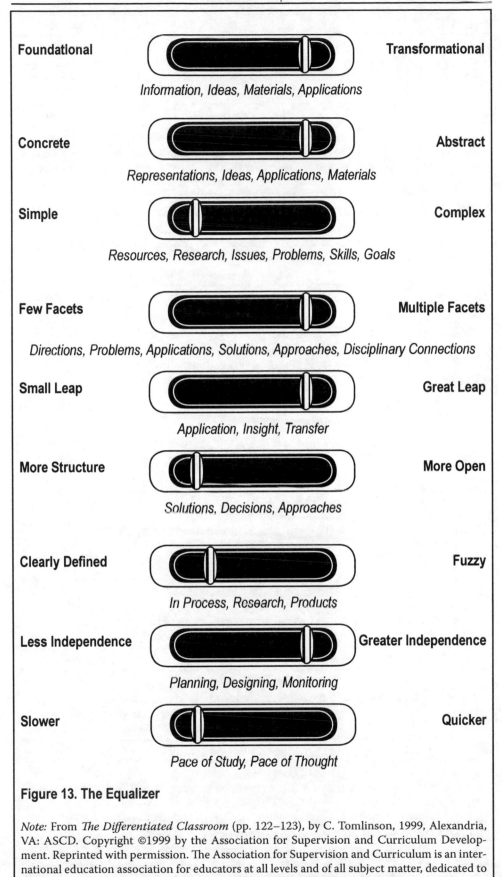

Foundatlonal — **Transformational**
Information, Ideas, Materials, Applications

Concrete — **Abstract**
Representations, Ideas, Applications, Materials

Simple — **Complex**
Resources, Research, Issues, Problems, Skills, Goals

Few Facets — **Multiple Facets**
Directions, Problems, Applications, Solutions, Approaches, Disciplinary Connections

Small Leap — **Great Leap**
Application, Insight, Transfer

More Structure — **More Open**
Solutions, Decisions, Approaches

Clearly Defined — **Fuzzy**
In Process, Research, Products

Less Independence — **Greater Independence**
Planning, Designing, Monitoring

Slower — **Quicker**
Pace of Study, Pace of Thought

Figure 13. The Equalizer

Note: From *The Differentiated Classroom* (pp. 122–123), by C. Tomlinson, 1999, Alexandria, VA: ASCD. Copyright ©1999 by the Association for Supervision and Curriculum Development. Reprinted with permission. The Association for Supervision and Curriculum is an international education association for educators at all levels and of all subject matter, dedicated to the success of all learners. To learn more, visit ASCD at http://www.ascd.org.

Foundational							Transformational

Information, Ideas, Materials, Applications
Students still struggling with key concepts will need content and activities that are foundational while students who already grasp key principles and skills need to work with materials that will allow them to modify, transform, or adapt their understanding.

Concrete							Abstract

Representations, Ideas, Applications, Materials
Students who are unclear about key concepts or skills need more tangible, hands-on, and/or real world examples which are straightforward while those who are more advanced in their understanding can work with implications or extensions of the ideas.

Simple							Complex

Resources, Research, Issues, Problems, Skills, Goals
Students who are unclear about key concepts or skills need more tangible, hands-on, and/or real world examples which are straightforward while those who are more advanced in their understanding can work with implications or extensions of the ideas.

Few Facets							Multiple Facets

Directions, Problems, Applications, Solutions, Approaches, Disciplinary Connections
Students who have a more basic understanding of the material may need few steps, fewer directions or fewer connections, while those with more advanced understanding will need multi-step problems, more connections among disciplines and more complex directions.

Small Leap							Great Leap

Application, Insight, Transfer
Students who are struggling to make meaning out of the content need assistance with applying or transferring the ideas while more advanced learners can make greater leaps of application to complete a task.

More Structure							More Open

Solutions, Decisions, Approaches
Less advanced learners may need more scaffolding to complete a particular task, while more advanced learners may be given a more open-ended task.

Clearly Defined							Fuzzy

In Process, Research, Products
Less advanced learners may work better with problems that have few unknowns, are more algorithmic, and less ambiguous while more advanced learners are challenged by problems with less clarity, more unknowns, extraneous data, and more heuristic.

Less Independence							Greater Independence

Planning, Designing, Monitoring
Students who require more precise directions, more modeling, and/or more guidance with time management and planning may not work well independently, while students who need less adult guidance, who set goals and manage time wisely, may work more independently.

Slower							Quicker

Pace of Study, Pace of Thought
Less advanced students may be able to handle more complex material if they are given more time, while more advanced learners may benefit from a quicker pace of study and thought. It may be necessary to slow the pace for advanced learners when they wish to pursue a topic in more depth.

Figure 14. Thinking about differentiation—The Equalizer: A continuum of choices

Note. Adapted from "Good Teaching for One and All: Does Gifted Education Have an Instructional Identity," by C. A. Tomlinson, 1997, *Journal for the Education of the Gifted, 20,* 155–174. Reprinted with permission.

Chapter 7

Template

Template With Guiding Questions

The following are some questions to ask yourself as you develop a lesson. A template is included as Figure 15.

Subject:
- For what subject am I writing the lesson?
- Does this lesson integrate more than one subject?

Grade:
- What grade level does this lesson target?
- Is this a multigrade level lesson?

Standard:
- What national standard is being addressed?
- Are there state and/or local standards that should be addressed?
- Are there standards specific to the school that must be addressed?

Key Concept:
- What "Big Idea" am I targeting?
- Why am I teaching this concept?
- Does this concept follow from the standard?
- Are there other concepts that will be addressed tangentially in the lesson?

Subject:

Grade:

Standard:

Key Concept:

Essential Understanding:

Background:

Tiered in (choose one) Content, Process, or Product

Tiered in according to (choose one) Readiness, Interest, or Learning Profile

Tier I:

Tier II:

Tier III:

Assessment:

Figure 15. Template for planning tiered lessons

Essential Understanding:
- Does this essential understanding follow from the key concept?
- What do I want the students to know at the end of the lesson regardless of their placement in the tiers?
- Why should my students learn this?

Background:
- What scaffolding is necessary?
- What material must have already been covered?
- What must the students have already learned?
- Are there other skills that must be taught first?
- Where does this lesson fit in the unit?
- What background information do I need to know to teach the lesson?
- Is there information from other sources that I can use to enhance the lesson?

Tiered in (choose one) Content, Process, or Product
- Should this lesson be tiered in content (what I want the students to learn)?
- Should this lesson be tiered in process (the way students make sense out of the content)?
- Should this lesson be tiered in product (the outcome at the end of a lesson, lesson set, or unit)?

Tiered According to (choose one) Readiness, Interest, or Learning Profile
- Is it best to tier this lesson based on the ability level of the students (readiness)?
- Is it best to tier this lesson based on the students' attraction to various topics (interest)?
- Is it best to tier this lesson based on the students' preference for a particular learning style (learning profile)?

Tiers:
- Using pretests or other preassessment criteria, how many tiers will be needed?
- If I choose to tier on readiness, how many ability groups do I have for this lesson?
- If I choose to tier on readiness, did I use the Equalizer to help adjust the activities in each tier?
- If I choose to tier on interest, will I control the number of tiers by limiting choices or should I allow free choice?
- If I choose to tier on learning profile, which learning styles model will I use?

- Are the activities for each tier equally engaging?
- Are the activities moderately challenging for the students in the tier?

Assessment:
- Will I use formative assessment, summative assessment, or both?
- Have I chosen a variety of ways to assess student work?
- Do I need to develop a rubric, test, or other means of assessment?
- Does the assessment need to be differentiated?

Chapter 8

Resources

The list below contains resources we have found useful for learning more about differentiation and preparing lessons.

Curriculum Writing

Erickson, H. L. (2001). *Stirring the head, heart, and soul: Redefining curriculum and instruction* (2nd ed.). Thousand Oaks, CA: Corwin Press.

Erickson, H. L. (2002). *Concept-based curriculum and instruction*. Thousand Oaks, CA: Corwin Press.

Classroom Management

Cummings, C. (2000). *Winning strategies for classroom management*. Alexandria, VA: Association for Supervision and Curriculum Development.

Marzano, R. J. (2003). *Classroom management that works*. Alexandria, VA: Association for Supervision and Curriculum Development.

McLeod, J., Fisher, J., & Hoover, G. (2003). *The key elements of classroom management*. Alexandria, VA: Association for Supervision and Curriculum Development.

Differentiated Instructional Strategies

Gregory, G. H. (2003). *Differentiated instructional strategies in practice*. Thousand Oaks, CA: Corwin Press.

Gregory, G. H., & Chapman, C. (2002). *Differentiated instructional strategies.* Thousand Oaks, CA: Corwin Press.

Heacox, D. (2002). *Differentiating instruction in the regular classroom.* Minneapolis, MN: Free Spirit Publishing.

Reis, S. M., Burns, D. E., & Renzulli, J. S. (1992). *Curriculum compacting.* Mansfield Center, CT: Creative Learning Press.

Tomlinson, C. A. (1999). *The differentiated classroom: Responding to the needs of all learners.* Alexandria, VA: Association for Supervision and Curriculum Development.

Tomlinson, C. A. (2001). *How to differentiate instruction in mixed-ability classrooms* (2nd ed.). Alexandria, VA: Association for Supervision and Curriculum Development.

Tomlinson, C. A. (2003). *Fulfilling the promise of the differentiated classroom.* Alexandria, VA: Association for Supervision and Curriculum Development.

Tomlinson, C. A., & Eidson, C. C. (2003). *Differentiation in practice: A resource guide for differentiating curriculum, grades K–5.* Alexandria, VA: Association for Supervision and Curriculum Development.

Winebrenner, S. (2000). *Teaching gifted kids in the regular classroom* (Rev. ed.). Minneapolis, MN: Free Spirit Publishing.

Learning Profile

Butler, K. A. (1990). *Learning and teaching style: In theory and practice.* Columbia, CT: Gregorc Associates.

Campbell, L., Campbell, B., & Dickinson, D. (2003). *Teaching and learning through multiple intelligences* (3rd ed.). Boston: Allyn & Bacon.

Dunn, R. (1996). *How to implement and supervise a learning style program.* Alexandria, VA: Association for Supervision and Curriculum Development.

Hutcheson, C. (1999). *Learning style questionnaire.* Amherst, MA: HRD Press.

Lawrence, G. (1979). *People types and tiger stripes: A practical guide to learning styles.* Gainesville, FL: Center for Applications of Psychological Type.

Renzulli, J. (2002). *Learning styles inventory version III: A measure of student preferences for instructional techniques.* Mansfield Center, CT: Creative Learning Press.

Silver, H., Strong, R., & Perini, M. (2000). *So each may learn: Integrating learning styles and multiple intelligences.* Alexandria, VA: Association for Supervision and Curriculum Development.

Vail, P. L. (1992). *Learning styles: Food for thought and 130 practical tips for teachers K–4.* Rosemont, NJ: Modern Learning Press.

Differentiated Assessment

General

Arter, J., & McTighe, J. (2001). *Scoring rubrics in the classroom.* Thousand Oaks, CA: Corwin Press.

Costa, A. L., & Kallick, B. (2004). *Assessment strategies for self-directed learning.* Thousand Oaks, CA: Corwin Press.

Fogarty, R. (1999). *Balanced assessment.* Thousand Oaks, CA: Corwin Press.

Herman, J. L., Aschbacher, P. R., & Winters, L. (1992). *A practical guide to alternative assessment.* Alexandria, VA: Association for Supervision and Curriculum Development.

Johnson, D. W., & Johnson, R. T. (2004). *Assessing students in groups.* Thousand Oaks, CA: Corwin Press.

Kingore, B. (1999). *Assessment: Time-saving procedures for busy teachers* (2nd ed.). Austin, TX: Professional Associates.

Popham, W. J. (2005). *Classroom assessment: What teachers need to know* (4th ed.). Boston: Pearson Education.

Wiggins, G. P. (1999). *Assessing student performance.* San Francisco: Jossey-Bass.

Web Sites

- http://www.bsu/gate—Provides a list of resources that have great anchoring activities; also provides guidance for tiering lessons.
- http://www.ldpride.nct—Provides two good interactive instruments for determining a student's learning profile.
- http://www.doe.state.in.us/exceptional/gt/tiered_curriculum/welcome.html—Provides tiered lessons in language arts, mathematics, and science.
- http://www.CurriculumProject.com—Provides a link to the StandardWriter rubric software.
- http://www.inspiration.com—Provides various tools to build graphic organizers and includes a free trial of its software.

Chapter 9

Examples

This chapter is divided into two sections, one with individual lessons and the other with mini-units comprised of multiple lessons. These sample lessons and mini-units can be used "as is" if appropriate for your students or can be modified to meet your own classroom needs. Keep in mind that although a grade level is specified you shouldn't think of it as an absolute, but rather as a place to start. The nature of tiered lessons makes most of them usable at a number of grade levels. However, tiered lessons are developed based on a particular set of students, so you may need to remove and/or add tiers for your set of students. We have included the national standards for each subject area from the appropriate national organization (e.g., National Council of Teachers of Mathematics (NCTM) for math lessons). You may want to identify your state standard that matches the national standard we have selected. The lessons in this book have been field tested in a number of academically diverse elementary classrooms.

Keep in mind that lessons, worksheets, and other materials do not need to be developed from scratch. Several of the examples that follow use activities from resource books and materials, as well as trade books, to develop the various tiers. The intention here is not to reinvent the wheel. In this way, the time it takes to create an appealing, engaging tiered lesson or unit is used more effectively and efficiently.

Individual Lessons

Section 1: Lessons Tiered According to Readiness

When tiering in content according to readiness, you are addressing the ability level of your students, which means you need to have a way of determining each student's level. One possible way is to pretest on the material. Many textbooks have prepared preassessments for each chapter that can be used as a pretest. To create your own pretest, select or formulate questions that address the major facts and concepts for the material pertaining to this lesson. It is important that a pretest not be lengthy in the number of questions or the time to take the test. Be sure students understand the pretest will be used as an indicator of what they already know and will not count toward their grade. Determine what you will consider as mastery of the content, for example, a score above 85%, and place your students in tiers accordingly. Those who score below 60% would be placed in the first tier, those who receive between 60% and 85% would be placed in the next tier, and those who receive above 85% would be placed in the advanced tier. You should determine the percentages for each pretest depending on whether this is brand new material, material covered in a previous grade, or material that should have been previously mastered.

The mathematics lesson that follows is tiered in content according to readiness. Note that each tier works with a set of different fractions, going from familiar fractions to those that are unfamiliar. However, each tier uses the same process to complete the lesson and make sense of its set of fractions. The social studies lesson that follows is also tiered in content according to readiness. It illustrates how to take a commercially available game and tier it by modifying the rules. The language arts lesson is tiered in content by using a different book for each tier.

The science lesson that follows is tiered in process according to readiness. Process is the way in which students make sense of or practice the content. There are a number of science process skills that students may use when conducting investigations. In this lesson, students make sense of the content by using processes that move from concrete to abstract and from simple to complex. Students are placed in tiers according to their ability to deal with abstractness, which the teacher has determined by observing the students in previous investigations and activities.

Tiering the product of a lesson on readiness may be approached in different ways. One way would be to have students create similar products, but vary the number and types of materials used by each tier. Another approach would be to have students create different products that vary in their complexity from one tier to another. As with any readiness tiering, remember that the tiers should be *qualitatively* different. It is inappropriate to require the advanced students to do quantitatively more while the other students are required to do less. The bottom line is that products should be a means for all students to apply and extend the content.

Sample Tiered Lesson 1

Understanding Fractions: Grade 1

Subject: Mathematics

Grade: First

Standard: All students will understand numbers, ways of representing numbers, relationships among numbers, and number systems.

Key Concept: Students will develop an understanding of simple fractions.

Essential Understanding: Students will illustrate how fractions represent part of a whole.

Background: Fractions (halves/thirds) have been introduced and illustrated by the students with pictures. Available materials should include paper circles, squares, rectangles, and triangles. You may want to place pictures of specific items to go with each shape, such as pizza or birthday cake for large circles, Reese's© Peanut Butter Cups for small circles, sandwiches and subs for squares and rectangles, and pieces of pie for triangles. You could use pictures from magazines or from a clip art software program.

Tier I:
Using paper circles (pizzas) and squares (sandwiches), in pairs students will determine how to share the food equally and illustrate this by folding the paper. Have two pairs determine how they can share equally with four people. They can cut the parts and stack them to see if they match. Have the quad repeat the process for sharing a Reese's© Peanut Butter Cup equally with three people.

Tier II:
Using paper circles (pizzas) and squares (sandwiches), in triads students will determine how to share the food equally and illustrate this by folding the paper. Have two triads determine how they can share equally with six people. Have the group of six repeat the process for sharing a birthday cake with 12 people. In each case, they can cut the parts and stack to match. Have the group start with half a cake and divide it equally for 3, 6, and 12 people.

Tier III:

Using paper rectangles (sandwiches) and triangles (slices of pie), in pairs the students will determine how to share the food in three different ways to get equal parts. Have them illustrate this by folding the paper. Are there different ways to divide each shape equally? How many ways are there? Have the pair determine which shapes—circles, squares, rectangles, triangles—are easier to divide evenly and illustrate why with a particular food of their choice.

Assessment: As children complete the activities note in your flip card chart their abilities to divide materials into equal parts and to recognize and check for equal parts. Ask yourself, can the child explain how many equal parts there are and show how he or she knows the parts are equal?

Figure 16. A student folds paper to learn about fractions.

Note. When this mathematics lesson was taught, the students were engaged during the entire lesson. The lesson was introduced by reading the book, *Eating Fractions* (McMillan, 1991). Students were placed in groups based on their level of readiness to interact with the content. Four students did not have a clear understanding of halves and fourths. These students needed a more concrete activity and were placed in Tier I. Another 12 students could recognize halves and thirds and were ready to complete the Tier II activity. They were placed in four triads. Two students had in-depth knowledge of halves and thirds and were placed in Tier III. This pair worked at a more abstract level and the questions that were asked required them to use different critical thinking skills than the other two groups. Tier I and Tier II students were provided with activities from the book, *Fractions* (Watt, 2001), to use as anchoring activities if they finished early or were waiting for the teacher's assistance. The anchor for Tier III students was *Apple Fractions* (Pallotta, 2002), which introduced fifths through tenths.

Sample Tiered Lesson 2
Using Maps: Grade 4

Subject: Social Studies

Grade: Fourth

Standard: Theme 3: People, Places, and Environments

Key Concept: Students will develop an understanding of relative location, direction, size, and shape through the use of maps.

Essential Understanding: Students will be able to construct a mental map to readily locate and identify locales, regions, and states.

Background: Students have been studying the United States. They have learned the names of each state and its capital and have spent time locating the states on maps. This lesson should be used as a culminating review activity prior to the unit test. Students who can readily identify states on an outline map of the U.S. with state names removed will work in Tier II. Students who still need assistance locating states on this type of map will work in Tier I. Students should work in groups of two to four.

Tier I:
Students will play the USA Edition of the game BORDERLINE™ according to the regular rules of play. The object of the game is to be the first to get rid of all your cards that have a state on one side and a section of the U.S. map showing bordering states on the reverse side. Students may play a bordering state, a wildcard, or bluff. See game for further details. The game is available from http://www.borderlinegames.com

Tier II:
Students will play the USA Edition of the game BORDERLINE™ according to the regular rules of play except they cannot look at both sides of the card. Students keep all cards on the table and do not have the advantage of using the map showing bordering states.

Assessment: This lesson is self-checking and is meant to provide practice before the unit test, which will include locating states on a blank map and identifying capitals and bordering states.

Drawing Inferences: Grade 5

Subject: Reading

Grade: Fifth

Standard: Standard 3: Students apply a wide range of strategies to comprehend, interpret, evaluate, and appreciate texts.

Key Concept: Drawing inferences, conclusions, and generalizations are strategies that help the reader interpret texts.

Essential Understanding: Clues in a story allow the reader to draw inferences about outcomes.

Background: Students are already familiar with different kinds of graphic organizers. In this lesson, students will use a graphic organizer to help them uncover clues, make inferences, and determine actual outcomes. All students will use the same graphic organizer (see Figure 17). They will use different texts depending on their ability to handle abstraction. The students in Tier I use a text, *The Wretched Stone* (Van Allsburg, 1991), whose clues are not as subtle as the text, *The Stranger*, (Van Allsburg, 1986) used in Tier II. If there is not a classroom set of the two texts or enough texts are not available, you may choose to read the designated book to the students assigned to one tier while students placed in the other tier work on anchoring activities. Be sure the students fill in the graphic organizer as they read the story, not after they read the story.

If these two books are not available, other books by Chris Van Allsburg will generally work. The teacher will want to read the substitute books to be sure there are clues similar to those in the two selected works available.

Tier I:
Students will read the book, *The Wretched Stone*.

Tier II:
Students will read the book, *The Stranger*.

Assessment: The graphic organizers should be checked for accuracy. A whole class discussion about the use of clues for making inferences should follow.

The teacher may want to reread both books to the whole class as the graphic organizers are discussed. A follow-up activity could involve the use of graphic organizers to compare and contrast the plots of the books. If students have had experiences with making a hypothesis in science, the teacher may want to relate that concept to the process used in the texts.

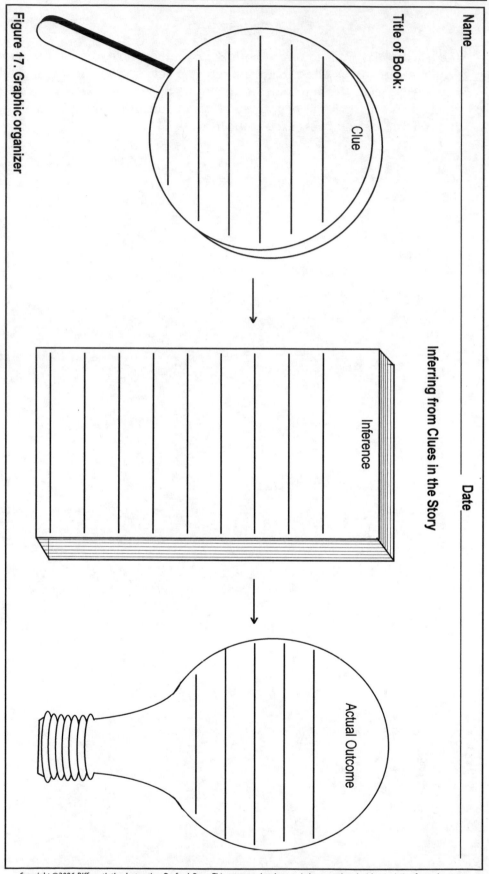

Name _____

Title of Book: _____

Date _____

Inferring from Clues in the Story

Clue

Inference

Actual Outcome

Figure 17. Graphic organizer

Sample Tiered Lesson 4
Needs of Plants: Grade 2

Subject: Science

Grade: Second

Standard: Content Standard C: All students should develop understanding of the characteristics of organisms.

Key Concept: Organisms have basic needs and can survive only in environments in which their needs can be met.

Essential Understanding: Plants need soil, sunlight, and water in order to grow.

Background: The students have already studied the needs of animals as part of their work with living things. The activity introduces a lesson that allows students to discover what is necessary for plants to grow. Students will use guided discovery to learn the needs of plants. Students who need step-by-step directions and more structure should work in Tier I. Tier II is less structured, and Tier III is the least structured.

All groups will be investigating the needs of plants. Available materials should include soil, water, cups, milk cartons or pots, seeds (some seeds that work well are radish, beans, or the Wisconsin FastPlants available from Carolina Biological Supply), metric ruler, metric measuring cup, and markers.

Tier I:
These students will be given step-by-step directions to perform an investigation that will assist them in determining what plants need in order to grow. Students will use the variables of soil, water, and sunlight to determine what plants need to live. Most science books will have a detailed step-by-step experiment with plants that can be used or you may choose to write out the directions.

Tier II:
These students will investigate the needs of plants by varying the amount of water given to the plants while keeping the amount of soil and sunlight constant. Provide directions for the students to begin the investigation (materials, how to plant, amount of soil to use, number of seeds per cup, etc.), but have them determine the number of cups they will use and how to vary the water in each cup.

Tier III:

These students will read *The Empty Pot* by Demi (1996) or another story that deals with the needs of plants. Students will design and carry out an investigation based on the story. Students should include their research question, hypothesis, materials, procedure, data collection, results, and conclusion. As students carry out their investigation, provide assistance as needed.

Assessment: The teacher will use a flip card chart to assess students' progress during the design and implementation of the investigations for formative assessment. Science journals and activity sheets that include the information necessary to replicate the investigation, as well as the data tables and conclusions serve as summative assessment. Appropriate results (e.g., plants grew, plants didn't grow) based on experimental conditions also serve as summative evaluation.

Section 2: Lessons Tiered According to Learning Profile

When tiering according to learning profile, you must first determine each student's learning preference. To determine learning preferences, you may use a checklist, rating scale, or questionnaire designed for that purpose. There are a number of resources that provide means for determining learning profiles of students. Some possible choices are listed in Chapter 8. In tiers based on learning profile, you will notice that students in each tier prefer the same learning style, but may have different abilities.

In the mathematics lesson that follows, students are grouped heterogeneously based on one of two learning preferences: kinesthetic or visual. Notice the activities are at relatively the same level of complexity. This would be the layer cake model as opposed to the wedding cake model used when tiering according to readiness. A good resource for information about learning profiles in teaching math is Mark Wahl's *Math for Humans: Teaching Math Through 8 Intelligences* (1999).

In the science lesson, students are grouped according to three of Gardner's eight multiple intelligences: verbal-linguistic learners, logical-mathematical learners, and visual-spatial learners. Again, you will notice the activities are all at relatively the same level of complexity. A good resource for information about Gardner's naturalist intelligence for science is Glock, Wertz, and Meyer's *Discovering the Naturalist Intelligence: Science in the School Yard* (1998).

In the social studies lesson, students are grouped according to their learning style, which the teacher determined earlier in the year through a learning styles inventory. Each group produces a different product at relatively the same level of challenge.

Congruency and Symmetry: Grade 3

Subject: Mathematics

Grade: Third

Standard: Students will analyze characteristics and properties of two- and three-dimensional geometric shapes and develop mathematical arguments about geometric relationships.

Key Concept: Students will work with geometric shapes and develop spatial sense.

Essential Understanding: Students will find congruent figures and identify lines of symmetry for a variety of objects.

Background: This would be the fourth or fifth lesson in a unit on geometry where the first few lessons have covered various geometric shapes, as well as slides, flips, turns, congruence, and symmetry.

Tier I: Kinesthetic Learners
Pairs of students will use brightly colored paper to make several simple origami designs. Provide guidance when necessary. When the students are finished, have them unfold the figure(s), find any congruent shapes, and identify lines of symmetry. Students will share the origami figures and have classmates try to construct them. See *Origami Math*, Grades 2–3 (2004a) and Grades 4–6 (2004b) published by Scholastic (Baicker, 2004a, 2004b) for specific origami designs that lend themselves to this age group.

Tier II: Visual Learners
Pairs of students will work with pictures of items from nature, such as butterflies, sunflowers, rainbows, snowflakes, and starfish. Students will find any congruent shapes and identify lines of symmetry for each item. Students then color the pictures to help show the lines of symmetry. Students will cut out the figures and have classmates find the lines of symmetry.

Assessment: Use a summative assessment, such as a test, to determine students' abilities to identify the congruent shapes and lines of symmetry. Have each student reflect in writing about congruent shapes and lines of symmetry. From a list of objects in the classroom, students will select an object and write about whether or not the object has congruent parts and/or lines of symmetry and why. The students could also include a drawing that illustrates the congruent parts and/or lines of symmetry. These reflections should be graded for accuracy, grammar, and spelling.

Sample Tiered Lesson 6
Solar System Museum: Grade 4

Subject: Science

Grade: Fourth

Standard: Content Standard D: All students should develop an understanding of Earth in the solar system.

Key Concept: Earth is the third planet from the sun in a system that includes the moon, the sun, eight other planets and their moons, and smaller objects, such as asteroids and comets.

Essential Understanding: Objects in the solar system exist in a variety of sizes, shapes, and colors, and scale models are often used to represent objects that are very large or very far away.

Background: Students have been studying the solar system and other objects in space. They have covered the nightly and yearly movement of stars in the sky, scientists' use of different tools to study a variety of objects in the sky, and Earth's place in the solar system and its relationship to the sun, moon, and other planets. As a culmination of that study, students will make a Solar System museum.

Each group will contribute to the conception, design, and assembling of the museum. Other classes, parents, and community members may be invited to visit the museum. Each tier's task is based on a particular intelligence as identified by Howard Gardner (refer to Chapter 4 and Chapter 8 for information on Gardner's multiple intelligences); however, it will take cooperation from all three tiers to make the museum successful.

Available materials should include:

- poster board (white and colored),
- markers (broad and fine tip),
- string (preferably transparent plastic thread),
- glue,
- tape,
- glue gun (needs adult supervision),
- glitter,
- spray paint (use outside) or tempera paint,
- Styrofoam,

- books on stars in general,
- supplemental material for research,
- access to the Internet for research,
- calculators,
- grid paper,
- compass,
- protractor, and
- other materials as needed.

Depending on the sophistication of your class, you may want to stick with only planets and their moons, as well as the sun. However, if students are able, adding in asteroids, comets, and other objects will enhance the museum.

Tier I: Verbal-Linguistic Learners

Students in this tier will write the museum cards that identify the planet, information about the planet, and the name of any moons belonging to the planet. Depending on the sophistication of your students, you may need to prepare a list of the categories of information they must address, such as color, size, and temperature. You may prefer to give the students a rubric that addresses the areas of assessment for this task including accuracy of information, neatness of lettering on placard (or use of a word processing program), and readability. They will plan the guide for the museum.

Tier II: Logical-Mathematical Learners

Students working at this tier will need to research the size of the various planets and moons to plan the appropriate scale for the museum. They will need to have calculators available for this task. You may need to brief this tier with a mini-lesson on scale if they have not covered this yet. Grid paper is also helpful. They will need to make a chart that includes the name of the planet and its moons, actual sizes, and scale sizes. They will need to act as technical consultants to the Visual-Spatial tier during the construction of the models. A rubric that addresses mathematical skills, scale, and accuracy would be a good assessment tool for this tier.

Tier III: Visual-Spatial Learners

Students working at this tier will construct three-dimensional models of the planets and their moons. They will consult with the Logical-Mathematical learners to plan for the size and type of material for each, and they will consult with the Verbal-Linguistics tier to determine any distinguishing characteristics for each. They will design, color, cut, and hang models of each planet and moon. A rubric for this tier would include criteria such as accuracy, appropriateness of design, neatness, and aesthetic quality.

Assessment: In addition to the rubric assessments mentioned within each tier, teacher observation and student interviews during group work may also be used. You may wish to use some means of gathering information from those who visit the museum, including suggestions for improvement.

Students should work together to prepare the museum and take turns acting as guides for the visitors. A whole class discussion about the project focusing on what was learned may be conducted prior to and again after visitors have been to the museum.

Sample Tiered Lesson 7

Fairness, Justice, and Equity: Grade 2

Subject: Social Studies

Grade: Second

Standard: Theme 6: Power, Authority, and Governance

Key Concept: The study of how people create and change structures of power, authority, and governance contributes to concepts such as fairness, equity, and justice.

Essential Understanding: Students recognize and give examples of the tensions between the wants and needs of individuals and groups, and concepts such as fairness, equity, and justice.

Background: The teacher will read *The Story of Ruby Bridges* by Robert Coles (1995) to the whole class followed by a class discussion of the major points of the story. Earlier in the year, the teacher created learning profiles of her students using various learning styles instruments and checklists. The teacher has referred to this information to create the groups for this lesson. Each tier has several groups of 3–4 students. For example, in Tier I the teacher has formed two groups of four students. Each group will plan and carry out its own interview, including the questions that will be asked and the people who will be interviewed. Although each tier has a different product, the teacher should emphasize that the concepts of justices, fairness, and equity should be addressed.

Tier I: Verbal-Linguistic Learners
Students in this tier will create a "60 Minutes" type news segment or an interview to be broadcast on the nightly news. Students may need a mini-lesson on interviewing skills. Students may want to set up an interview area and may need to borrow a microphone.

Tier II: Musical-Rhythmic Learners
Students working at this tier will create a rap to tell the story of Ruby Bridges and design their own instruments to accompany the rap. Students in this tier will need access to materials that can be used to make simple instruments, such as beans, rice, empty oatmeal containers, boxes, rubber bands, empty metal cans, and other similar items.

Tier III: Bodily-Kinesthetic Learners
Students working at this tier will depict several scenes from the story using miming. Students may need a mini-lesson on how to mime. Students need to understand that only nonverbal communication, such as gesturing, changing expressions, and movement, is allowed. Depending on the wishes of the groups and the approval of the teacher, students in this tier may want to work in larger groups to make their scenes more vivid.

Assessment: Each product is different and will require a different rubric. Rubrics should address the elements unique to each product, as well as elements of the book, including the concepts of justice, equity, and fairness. While each group is working the teacher should visit each one and note which students have a good grasp of the concepts and which students may need additional work for mastery. All groups will share their work with the class so that everyone has a chance to learn about the concepts of fairness, justice, and equity from different viewpoints and through different means of expression.

Section 3: Lessons Tiered According to Interest

When tiering lessons on interest, you may need to develop an interest inventory for your unit or lesson. This allows you to know ahead of time the students' preferences for the various topics you will cover. Knowing students' preferences ahead of time allows you to plan for your groups. However, you may decide not to use an interest inventory and instead allow students to make their choice at the time of the lesson. It is advisable to limit the number of choices you provide for students.

In the mathematics lesson, which has a product tiered on interest, the choices are teacher controlled and student selected. In the science lesson, which has the content tiered on interest, the teacher may let students have free choice as to which biome they will study, or the teacher may choose to preselect specific biomes and have students choose from those. The number of tiers will equal the number of choices. This lesson is illustrated with three tiers. Notice that the science lesson uses trade books, which are readily available, rather than having the teacher make materials for each tier. In the language arts lesson on haiku, a trade book is used as the introduction to this type of poetry. Students then choose the topic for their own haiku collection based on their interest.

Three-Dimensional Objects: Kindergarten

Subject: Mathematics

Grade: Kindergarten

Standard: The students will recognize, name, build, draw, compare, and sort two- and three-dimensional shapes.

Key Concept: Some three-dimensional shapes can be built with blocks.

Essential Understanding: The students will use blocks of varying sizes to replicate three-dimensional objects (e.g., cubes and rectangular prisms).

Background: Before beginning this lesson, students should be able to sort two-dimensional shapes. Available materials should include two groups of three-dimensional objects or pictures of objects from two areas, such as animals and plants or buildings and tools, and sets of blocks in a variety of sizes, shapes, and colors. Students will select a set of objects that interest them the most.

Tier I:
Given at least four 3-D objects or pictures of animals, students build a replica of at least two of the objects using a set of blocks. Students will share their creations with each other and the teacher.

Tier II:
Given at least four 3-D objects or pictures of plants, students build a replica of at least two of the objects using a set of blocks. Students will share their creations with each other and the teacher.

Assessment: Using a flip card chart, the teacher can note observations while students are creating their replicas and gather student responses to questioning about similarities and differences from the given set of objects. Note these are types of formative assessment appropriate for this lesson.

Biomes: Grade 5

Subject: Science

Grade: Fifth

Standard: Content Standard C: All students should develop understanding of populations and ecosystems.

Key Concept: For any particular environment, some kinds of plants and animals survive well, some do not survive well, and others cannot survive at all.

Essential Understanding: Animals are adapted to a particular environment.

Background: This lesson is part of a unit on different water biomes. Students have studied the basic needs of animals and are familiar with vocabulary such as niche, survival of the fittest, environment, biome, and food chain. Students are placed in tiers according to their interest in one of three water biomes: estuary, river, or lake. A good series of books that address water biomes are *Biomes of North America, Set II*, by Rebecca L. Johnson (2004). Indicated below are appropriate books for each tier from the series.

Tier I: *A Journey Into an Estuary* (ISBN: 0822520451)
Tier II: *A Journey Into a River* (ISBN: 0822520443)
Tier III: *A Journey Into a Lake* (ISBN: 0822520435)

Each group should make a chart listing names of various animals that live in each biome across the top and characteristics/needs of the animal down the side. Examples include movement, body covering, body temperature, number of eyes, number of ears, number of legs, type of food eaten, how they get water, and shelter. Use at least 10 animals per group, and use more if students are able. Once the chart is completed, each student should choose two animals to research and study in depth, preparing a list of information about how each animal catches its food, makes a living area, defends itself, and so on. More advanced students could complete a compare and contrast diagram of their animals. Once the chart and the in-depth studies are completed, have students come together in a large group for sharing.

Assessment: Teacher observation during the group work, as well as individual interviews will serve as assessment. Have each group share the information on their charts, as well as the in-depth studies of the different animals. Have students compare and contrast the animals in the different biomes, and then lead them in a discussion of how animals are adapted. Ask if a specific animal (e.g., oystercatcher) could live in a different environment (river). Have them give reasons for their answers. The charts and in-depth studies are a nice transition to the concept of the five kingdom classification system. Students can work in groups to classify the animals they studied.

Sample Tiered Lesson 10
Haiku: Grade 3

Subject: Language Arts—Poetry

Grade: Third

Standard: Standard 6: Students apply knowledge of language structure, language conventions, media techniques, figurative language, and genre to create, critique, and discuss print materials.

Key Concept: For any genre, there are particular elements that distinguish that genre from others.

Essential Understanding: Haiku is a form of traditional Japanese poetry that consists of three lines of 5-7-5 units each.

Background: Students have been studying different forms of poetry. The teacher introduces the concept of haiku poetry through the book, *If Not for the Cat*, by Jack Prelutsky (2004). In this book the author presents 17 haiku with beautiful illustrations. In each haiku, a different animal is presented in such a way that the reader must figure out the name of the animal. One way to introduce this form of poetry would be to read several selections to the students or have them take turns reading and deciding what animal is being described. Then students could "clap" the syllables in each line to discover the convention used to write haiku. The Wikipedia Web site at http://en.wikipedia.org is a good place to find some basic information about haiku and its history. Tiers are formed by having students choose the category they will use to write their own haiku. The completed product would be an illustrated booklet of haiku related to the same category. Three categories have been provided as examples, but the teacher should feel free to adjust the categories according to the interests of the students in the classroom.

Tier I: Haiku will focus on sports.
Tier II: Haiku will focus on plants.
Tier III: Haiku will focus on food.

Assessment: Teacher observation during the group work, as well as individual interviews will serve as formative assessment. A rubric should be developed for evaluating the final product. Criteria should include items such as correct spelling and punctuation, adherence to the 5-7-5 rule, creativity, and appropriateness of illustrations.

Mini-Units

The two mini-units that follow were developed collaboratively with teachers to use in their own classrooms. Each unit took several weeks to plan, design, and prepare the materials to be used by the students. The number of tiers was based on preassessment by the teachers of the students who were enrolled in their classes. Student abilities ranged from developmentally delayed to highly able. Thus, in each case, it was appropriate to develop activities for three tiers. The number of students in each class varied between 16 and 20. Keep in mind, when using these mini-units you may need to modify them to meet the needs of the students in your classroom. Note that the lessons follow the template discussed in Chapter 7.

The Rock Unit was developed for use with second graders. It is a 2-week integrated math and science unit about rocks with three team lessons—introduction, tiered activity, and culminating group activity. The teachers actually began preparations several weeks in advance by having two guest speakers from the Indiana State Department of Transportation, a geologist and a trainer, who spoke about rocks and brought large samples. It would probably be better to have them visit closer to the beginning of the unit; however, the timing of this visit was determined by the schedule of the guest speakers. During the first week of the unit, the students constructed and decorated rock journals, and the teachers assisted the students in setting up two experiments: One group started to grow alum and sugar crystals, and the second group immersed sponge "bones" in an Epsom salts solution. The week following the unit students responded to the journal prompt, "Here is what I have learned about rocks . . ."

The Simple Machine Unit was developed for use with fourth graders. An initial version of this unit was developed with teachers and field tested with second graders. The unit presented here has been expanded and the level of difficulty increased. It is a 4-day unit about simple machines with an introductory day, two tiered activity days, and a culminating group activity day. One tiered activity uses trade books and the other a resource book of investigations.

Rock Unit: Grade 2

Subject: Science/Mathematics

Grade: Second

Science Standard: Content Standard B: All students should develop an understanding of properties of objects and materials.

Mathematics Standards: The students will understand measurable attributes of objects and the units, systems, and processes of measurement and apply appropriate techniques, tools, and formulas to determine measurements.

Key Concept: Rocks, minerals, and crystals are found throughout the Earth.

Essential Understanding: Attributes of rocks, minerals, and crystals help us identify them. They can be massed, measured, and sorted.

Background: The students have been divided into two groups to do experiments. One group has started to grow alum and sugar crystals. The second group has immersed sponge "bones" in an Epsom salts solution to show how minerals may be deposited to form fossilized bone. Directions for the experiments can be found in a book by Cindy Blobaum, *Geology Rocks!* (1999). In addition, students can bring a favorite "mystery rock" from home.

Students have made Rock Journals with pages to record their observations. The journals also had pages with the writing prompts already provided and a page with the definitions for crystal, mineral, and rock. Students have made a first entry in the journal as a response to this prompt: What do you know about rocks, minerals, and crystals?

Each group will have a mini-lesson based on the activity the students will do in their tier. Tier I's lesson deals with how to use their senses, Tier II's lesson is on how to use an equal arm balance, and Tier III's lesson is on how to measure in centimeters with a ruler. While the teacher introduces one mini-lesson, the other students will work on their anchoring activities.

Day 1 is a whole class lesson to introduce the study of rocks, minerals, and crystals, while Day 2 is a tiered activity and Day 3 is a culminating group lesson.

Day 1: Whole Class Lesson

- Read *Rocks in His Head*, by Carol Otis Hurst (2001)
- Introduce vocabulary: rock, mineral, crystal.
- Look at samples under the microscope and view filmstrip. (We used our Intel Play™ QX3™ computer microscope and made a filmstrip of rocks, minerals, and crystals using the software provided with microscope.) If this equipment is not available, contact your local high school or state transportation department, either of whom may be able to loan you samples of rocks, minerals, and crystals.
- The students use Private Eye™ Loupes, similar to a jeweler's loupe, or a magnifying lens to observe their own fingers and then their "mystery rock."
- Students will draw their mystery rock in their journals, one picture with the loupe, one without.
- Determine if their mystery rock is a rock, mineral, or crystal.
- Tally sample types on the board.
- Ask students how they determined the sample was a rock, mineral, or crystal.

Day 2: Tiered Activity

This lesson is tiered in process according to readiness.

Before starting the activities, the students will review what they learned in Day 1, particularly the definitions of rock, mineral, and crystal. Students have had the opportunity to observe their experiments and write the observations in their Rock Journals. Rocks used by each tier were selected from rock sample kits available from Loose in the Lab (visit http://looseinthelab.com/products.htm). They may also use their own rock in the following activities.

Tier I: Below Grade Level
This group will complete the activity, "Sorting and Ordering Objects."

Tier II: Grade Level
This group will complete the activity, "Finding the Mass of an Object."

Tier III: Above Grade Level
This group will complete the activity, "Finding the Length, Width, and Height of an Object." (*Note*: Originally, we had Tier II measure length, width, and height and Tier III work with mass. When we taught the lesson to the first class, we realized we needed to reverse the tiers. Conceptually, for these students, the measurement activities were more difficult than finding the mass of an object.)

Figure 18. A group examines crystals.

Day 3: Culminating Group Lesson

- Read *Everybody Needs a Rock*, by Byrd Baylor (1974).
- Students write in journal about their mystery rock explaining why it is special.
- Have students make a diorama showing where they found their rock.
- individually look at their "mystery rock" under the microscope.

Assessment: Students will be assessed through teacher observation during the activities using a flip card chart. Answers to the Day 2 activities will be checked for accuracy using an answer key developed for these specific sample rocks. Both the journal and diorama will be assessed with rubrics. The rubric for the journal should include criteria such as neatness, clarity of description, inclusion of drawings, and completeness of answers. The diorama rubric should include criteria such as an accurate portrayal of where the rock was found, originality, and creative use of materials.

Sorting and Ordering Objects

Materials: A bag of rock samples

You are going to sort the samples in your bag several different ways.

Smoothest to Roughest
1. Take out all the samples from your bag.
2. Feel each sample.
3. Decide if it is smooth or rough.
4. Place your samples in order from smoothest to roughest.
5. Write the number of each sample in smoothest to roughest order on your worksheet.

Lightest to Heaviest
1. Hold each sample.
2. Decide if it is light or heavy.
3. Place your samples in order from lightest to heaviest.
4. Write the number of each sample in lightest to heaviest order on your worksheet.

Shortest to Tallest
1. Look at each sample.
2. Decide if it is short or tall.
3. Place your samples in order from shortest to tallest.
4. Write the number of each sample in shortest to tallest order on your worksheet.

Sorting and Ordering Objects, continued

Shortest to Longest

1. Look at each sample.
2. Decide if it is short or long in length.
3. Place your samples in order from shortest to longest in length.
4. Write the number of each sample in shortest to longest order on your worksheet.

Lightest to Darkest

1. Look at the color of each sample.
2. Decide if it is light or dark.
3. Place your samples in order from lightest to darkest in color.
4. Write the number of each sample in lightest to darkest order on your worksheet.

Compare your results with your partner.

Name _____ Date _____

Sorting and Ordering Objects

The sample number is in the white spot on your sample. Place the sample numbers in the correct order below.

Smoothest _____ **Roughest**

Lightest _____ **Heaviest**

Shortest _____ **Tallest**

Shortest _____ **Longest**

Lightest _____ **Darkest**

Name_____ Date_____

Finding the Mass of an Object

Materials: A bag of rock samples, a balance, plastic masses

Mass is the measure of the amount of matter in an object. Weight is the measure of the force of gravity on an object. On Earth, mass and weight are equal.

You are going to find the mass of each sample in your bag. Here is what you will do:

1. Take all the samples from your bag.
2. Estimate the mass of each sample and order the samples from lightest to heaviest.
3. Record the number on the rock in the appropriate place on the worksheet.
4. Now take one sample and place it in the red pan on the balance.
5. Choose a plastic mass and place it in the yellow pan.
6. Continue adding one mass at a time until both pans balance.
7. Add the number of grams printed on each plastic mass in the yellow pan and record the sum on your worksheet. The sum is the total mass of your sample.
8. Repeat Steps 1–7 for each sample in your bag.

Find the number in the white spot on your sample. Write the number in the blank below to show the order of your estimate of each sample's mass.

_____   _____   _____   _____

Lightest   **Heaviest**

Finding the Mass of an Object, continued

Fill out the chart below to show the results when you found the actual mass of each sample.

Sample Number	Mass

Find the number in the white spot on your sample. Write the number in the blank below to show the order for the actual mass of the samples.

_____   _____   _____   _____

Lightest   **Heaviest**

Did your estimate agree with your actual results?

Name_____ Date_____

Finding the Length, Width, and Height of an Object

Materials: A bag of rock samples, a ruler, masking tape

You are going to find the length, width, and height of each sample in your bag. Here is what you will do:

1. Take a sample from your bag.
2. Place the sample on a strip of tape.
3. Mark one end of the sample on the tape with your pencil.
4. Without moving the sample, make a mark on the tape at the other end of the sample.
5. With your ruler, measure the distance in centimeters (cm) between the two marks. This is the length of the sample. Record this number.
6. Give the sample a one-quarter turn.
7. Mark one side of the sample on the tape with your pencil.
8. Without moving the sample, make a mark on the tape at the other side of the sample.
9. With your ruler, measure the distance in cm between the two marks. This is the width of the sample. Record this number.
10. Turning the sample on its side, use the same method to measure the height of the object, and record this number on your worksheet.
11. Repeat Steps 1–10 for each sample in your bag.

Fill in the chart on the following page to show your results. The sample number is in the white spot on your sample.

Finding the Length, Width, and Height of an Object, continued

Sample Number	Length	Width	Height

Simple Machines Unit: Grade 4

Subject: Science

Grade: Fourth

Standard: Content Standard E: All students should develop an understanding about science and technology.

Key Concept: People have invented tools and techniques to solve problems. Simple machines make work easier.

Essential Understanding: Students will identify the following simple machines: lever, pulley, screw, wedge, wheel and axle, and inclined plane. Students will understand how a lever works.

Background: Students do not need any background information. Day 1 is a whole class lesson to introduce the idea of simple machines. Days 2 and 3 are tiered activities. Day 4 is a culminating group lesson.

Day 1: Whole Class Lesson

- Read *The Simple Story of the 3 Pigs & the Scientific Wolf,* by Mary Fetzner (2002).
- While reading the story, items depicted in the story should be shown to the students. Items readily available, such as a can opener or jar with screw lid, can be brought from home. Others items, such as a ladder or axe, can be shown using large pictures from a clip art software program.
- After the end of the story, hold up some of the simple machines that were featured in the story, as well as some additional examples of other simple machines, and ask students to explain how each item could make tasks easier.

Day 2: Tiered Activity

Introduce the simple machine using the *Early Bird Physics Books Series* (2001), by Sally M. Walker and Roseann Feldmann (*Inclined Planes and Wedges, Levers, Pulleys, Screws,* and *Wheels and Axles*).
This lesson is tiered in content according to interest.

- Divide the students into five groups according to their interest in learning about a specific simple machine.
- Distribute the appropriate book to the corresponding group.
- In each group, students read the book and prepare a poster indicating characteristics of the machine, examples, and how the machine helps make work easier than if it were done by hand. Have available resource material, such as other books on simple machines, magazines, and/or Internet access for gathering examples of machines.
- Share posters in whole group discussion.
- Display posters around the classroom for future reference.

Assessment: Student posters will be checked for accuracy. Students will then be given a copy of a Venn diagram to complete by using any two simple machines and the information available on the posters to compare and contrast them.

Day 3: Tiered Activity

The following is an investigation showing how a lever works. You may choose to include additional investigations for each of the simple machines. Students are divided into groups based on their math and language abilities to complete one of the following investigations. This lesson is tiered in process according to readiness.

Tier I: At or Below Grade Level

These students will work in groups of two or three to complete the investigation, "Living Lever-Limbs!" Student use their arms and weighted buckets to learn about fulcrum, effort, and load.

Tier II: Above Grade Level

These students will work in groups of three to complete the investigation, "Never Say Never When It Comes to a LEVER!" Students use the concept of smaller children balancing a larger child on a seesaw to understand fulcrum, effort, and load.

Detailed descriptions of these and other investigations, as well as worksheets can be found in *Best of WonderScience, Volume 2*, by American Chemical Society (2001), pages 241–252.

Assessment: Students will share the results of their investigations. Students' worksheets will be checked for accuracy. Students will be given a balance toy, such as a Torque Twister™, to see if they can make it balance on their finger using what they learned in the investigations.

Day 4: Culminating Group Lesson

This is a review of simple machines. Reread the story, *The Simple Story of the 3 Pigs & the Scientific Wolf.* Ask students to explain how each simple machine was used or misused. Ask students the following question, "Why do you think the wolf failed when he tried to capture the three pigs?"

Before beginning the activity, the groups from the Day 2 activity will have made a card that illustrates their simple machine.

- After reading the story, students will sit in a circle on the floor.
- In the center of the circle is a collection of everyday items that are simple machines.
- Have students take turns choosing an item and putting it beside the correct card. The student describes how the machine is used to make work easier.
- The other students determine whether the item was placed correctly and if the correct explanation was given. If everything is correct, another student takes a turn. If the item is not placed correctly or an incorrect explanation is given, the student may try again. If something is still incorrect, the item is returned to the collection.
- Students take turns until all the items have been correctly identified and their function explained.

This activity could also be developed as a learning center with a self-checking key.

References

Aardema, V. (1981). *Bringing the rain to Kapiti plai*n. New York: Dial Books.

American Chemical Society. (2001). *The best of WonderScience, volume 2*. Belmont, CA: Wadsworth/Thomson Learning.

Baicker, K. (2004a). *Origami math: Grades 2–3*. New York: Scholastic.

Baicker, K. (2004b). *Origami math: Grades 4–6*. New York: Scholastic.

Baylor, B. (1974). *Everybody needs a rock*. New York: Aladdin.

Baylor, B. (1975). *The desert is theirs*. New York: Aladdin.

Blobaum, C. (1999). *Geology rocks! 50 hands-on activities to explore the Earth*. Charlotte, VT: Williamson Publishing Company.

Campbell, L., Campbell, D., & Dickinson, D. (2003). *Teaching & learning through multiple intelligences* (3rd ed.). Boston: Allyn & Bacon.

Coles, R. (1995). *The story of Ruby Bridges*. New York: Scholastic.

Demi. (1996). *The empty pot*. New York: Henry Holt and Company.

Erickson, H. L. (2001). *Stirring the head, heart, and soul: Redefining curriculum and instruction* (2nd ed.). Thousand Oaks, CA: Corwin Press.

Evertson, C., Emmer, E., & Worsham, M. (2005). *Classroom management for elementary teachers* (7th ed.). Boston: Allyn & Bacon.

Fetzncr, M. (2000). *The simple story of the 3 pigs and the scientific wolf*. Marion, IL: Pieces of Learning.

Glock, J., Wertz, S., & Meyer, M. (1999). *Discovering the naturalist intelligence: Science in the school yard*. Tucson, AZ: Zephyr Press.

Hurst, C. O. (2001). *Rocks in his head*. New York: Greenwillow Books.

Johnson, R. L. (2004). *Biomes of North America, set II*. Minneapolis, MN: Lerner-Classroom.

McMillan, B. (1991). *Eating fractions*. New York: Scholastic.

National Council of Teachers of Mathematics (NCTM). (2000). *Principles and standards for school mathematics.* Reston, VA: Author.

National Research Council (NRC). (1996). *National science education standards.* Washington, DC: National Academy Press.

Pallotta, J. (2002). *Apple fractions.* New York: Scholastic.

Prelutsky, J. (2004). *If not for the cat.* New York: Greenwillow Books.

Rolheiser, C., Bower, B., & Stevahn, L. (2000). *The portfolio organizer.* Alexandria, VA: Association for Supervision and Curriculum Development.

Steptoe, J. (1972). *The story of jumping mouse.* New York: William Morrow.

Tomlinson, C. A. (1999). *The differentiated classroom: Responding to the needs of all learners.* Alexandria, VA: Association for Supervision and Curriculum Development.

Van Allsburg, C. (1986). *The stranger.* New York: Houghton Mifflin Company.

Van Allsburg, C. (1991). *The wretched stone.* New York: Houghton Mifflin Company.

Wahl, M. (1999). *Math for humans: Teaching math through 8 intelligences.* Langley, Washington: LivnLern Press.

Walker, S. M., & Feldmann, R. (2002). *Inclined planes and wedges.* Minneapolis, MN: Lerner Publications Group.

Walker, S. M., & Feldmann, R. (2002). *Levers.* Minneapolis, MN: Lerner Publications Group.

Walker, S. M., & Feldmann, R. (2002). *Pulleys.* Minneapolis, MN: Lerner Publications Group.

Walker, S. M., & Feldmann, R. (2002). *Screws.* Minneapolis, MN: Lerner Publications Group.

Walker, S. M., & Feldmann, R. (2002). *Wheels and axles.* Minneapolis, MN: Lerner Publications Group.

Watt, F. (2001). *Fractions.* New York: Scholastic.

About the Authors

Cheryll M. Adams is director of the Center for Gifted Studies and Talent Development at Ball State University. She also teaches graduate courses for certification in gifted education. For the past 25 years, she has served in the field of gifted education as a teacher of gifted students at all grade levels; as director of academic life at the Indiana Academy for Science, Mathematics, and Humanities; and as the principal teacher in the Ball State Institute for the Gifted in Mathematics program. Additionally, she has been the founder and director of various other programs for gifted students. Dr. Adams has authored or coauthored numerous publications in professional journals, as well as several book chapters. She serves on the editorial review board for *Roeper Review*, *Gifted Child Quarterly*, and the *Journal of Secondary Gifted Education*. She has served on the board of directors of the National Association for Gifted Children, has been president of the Indiana Association for the Gifted, and currently serves on the board of The Association for the Gifted, Council for Exceptional Children. In 2002, she received the NAGC Early Leader Award.

Rebecca L. Pierce is associate professor of Mathematical Sciences at Ball State University and a fellow at the Center for Gifted Studies and Talent Development. She teaches undergraduate and graduate courses in mathematics and statistics. For the last 30 years, Dr. Pierce has taught mathematics to elementary, middle school, high school, and college students. Dr. Pierce directs the Ball State Institute for the Gifted in Mathematics. Additionally, she worked as a senior research engineer for Bell Helicopter and as a statistical consultant for a variety of industries. She has authored or coauthored numerous publications in professional journals, as well as several book chapters. She is chair of Mathematics Day, a program for middle school girls interested in mathematics. She serves as a reviewer for *Roeper Review, Gifted Child Quarterly,* and the *Teacher Educator.* She received the Leadership Award from the Indiana Association for the Gifted in 2002.

Together, Dr. Adams and Dr. Pierce work with teachers throughout the United States and Europe toward establishing more effectively differentiated classrooms through the use of the CIRCLE MAP. In addition they provide professional development and consultation in the areas of mathematics, science, gifted identification, and program evaluation. They have coauthored and received two Javits grants from the federal government in partnership with the Indianapolis Public Schools.